AN ANALYTICAL STUDY OF THE LEGISLATIVE HISTORY OF THE NATIONAL FOOD SECURITY ACT (NFSA), 2013

VOLUME 2, ISSUE 1 OF BRILLOPEDIA

SANDRA ELIZABETH GEORGE AND SUPRIYA SATISH

Contents

Preface

"Start writing, no matter what. The water does not flow until the faucet is turned on".

• Louis L'Amour

Hundreds of students and professors are contributing their work to Brain Booster Articles, we are here to provide ample information about Law and Contemporary issues. Our aim is to provide a platform for today's generation to express their views and ideas on law and contemporary law.

Publication

This research paper is published in volume 2, issue 1 of Brillopedia

CHAPTER ONE

ABSTRACT

Hunger is an endless problem faced by the world. Some country or the other is driven to intermittent famines. Despite the huge incomes and development hunger remains a huge problem and one that is taking lives. Further hundreds of people around the world lead a life of insecurity and want. One of the major reasons for this problem is that many things are unclear about its characteristics, like the causation and possible remedies for it in the modern world.

Food security refers to the availability of necessary foodgrains to meet household demand as well as access, at the personal level, to adequate amounts of food at affordable prices.India is a signatory to The Universal Declaration of Human Rights[1] and International Covenant on Economic, Social and Cultural Rights,[2]which cast responsibilities on all State parties to recognize the right of everyone to adequate food.Additionally, the eradicating extreme poverty and hunger is also one of the goals under the Millennium Development Goals of the United Nations.[3]On a national level, the fundamental right to life which includes the right to food is enshrined in Article 21 of the Constitution of India. Furthermore, Article 47 of the Constitution under the Directive Principles of State Policy, provides that the State shall regard raising the level of nutrition, the standard of living and improving public health as its primary duties.

In lights of the said constitutional duties as well as the requirements under the international treaties, providing food security becamethe aim of the central government's schemes and policies as can be seen in Targeted Public Distribution System which provided free food to those below the poverty line.Despite this however, ensuring food security of the people, remained a challenge.To address this issue, the then President of India in her address to the Members of both the Houses of Parliament assembled together on 4[th]June 2009, announced that a new Act - the National Food

Security Act - will be enacted to provide a statutory basis for a framework which assures food security for all and entitle by law, every Below Poverty Line (BPL) family to 25 kg per month of rice or wheat atRs. 3/kg.The National Food Security Bill, 2011[4] ("Bill") was introduced in the LokSabha on 22nd December 2011. After incorporating various changes pursuant toParliamentary debates as well as the Parliamentary and Standing Committee Reports, a new bill[5] was drafted and passed into law on 12thSeptember 2013.

[1]UN General Assembly, *Universal Declaration of Human Rights*, 10 December 1948, 217A (III), https://www.refworld.org/docid/ 3ae6b3712c.html.

[2]UN General Assembly, *International Covenant on Civil and Political Rights*, 16 December 1966, United Nations, Treaty Series, vol. 999, p. 171, https://www.refworld.org/docid/3ae6b3aa0.html.

[3]The World Trade Organization, *Millenium Development Goals of the UN*, https://www5.worldbank.org/mdgs.

[4]*National Food Security Bill*, No. 132 of 2011, Bills of Parliament (India).

[5]*National Food Security Bill*, No. 109 of 2013, Bills of Parliament (India).

CHAPTER TWO

POLITICAL, DRAFTING, AND LEGAL ISSUES

The National Food Security Act, 2013 resulted from a social movement devoted to the actualization of the right to food in India. This campaign gained momentum after the People's Union for Civil Liberties filed a writ petition[1] in the Supreme Court in 2001 in the wake of a severe drought that struck many of the states in India.[2] The Right to Food Campaign demanded that the Public Distribution System (PDS) of India, which was highly targeted in nature to cater to the families below poverty line, be converted into a universal system where the poverty status of people would not be a criteria. The activists raised this issue because of the prevailing corruption and complication in determining the families below poverty line that hindered the PDS system from achieving its aim by leaving out those in need of the subsidies.[3] Though the final legislation did not create a universal PDS system as demanded by the activists, it still made a more inclusive one than what was present before by granting the same privileges to around three-fourths of the rural population and half of the urban population.

Another issue faced while drafting and enacting the National Food Security Act was that to ensure food security, it had to be assured that consumers have access to food products at an affordable rate. Still, at the same time, the concerns of the farmers about the prices at which they would sell their products also had to be protected. To balance the interests of both the farmers and consumers, it was decided that the government would purchase crops from the farmers, pay a minimum support price and then distribute them to the consumers through PDS. But this measure faced backlash from global organizations such as the World Trade Organisation (WTO), which follows a neoliberal policy that seeks to reduce government spending. The WTO has laid down the minimum support price (MSP) that can be given to the farmers under the WTO's Agreement on Agriculture (AoA) because it is a crucial trade policy. Those countries that provide an MSP higher than the given levels would attract sanctions because of their act of trade- distortion.[4] But to enact the NFSA, it was inevitable for India to show some resistance to the pressure from WTO. Finally, at the WTO meeting held in Bali in 2013, a temporary compromise was reached between the developing nations and WTO that it would not raise a dispute if a developing country is unable to meet the requirements under the AoA. But this was only until a permanent solution can be deliberated at the next conference.

Another issue raised was the high cost required to implement this Act. The Minister of Food had presented an understated amount as the cost when the Bill was introduced in the Parliament. But the supporters of the Act argued that the cost would not have to be borne by the government all at once; instead the implementation would happen over time, and so the cost should not be considered as an issue when the food security of a large number of the population was a more pressing issue at hand. There was also tension between the central government and the state governments concerning the coverage and cost relating to the Act. The Tamil Nadu government which has one of the best functioning PDS, protested against the exclusion of certain category people from the PDS system.[5]

[1]PUCL v. Union of India & Others, Civil Writ Petition, 196/2001.

[2]NandiniNayak, *Chasing Rights in Delhi: Social Movements and the National Food Security Act*, South Asia Multidisciplinary Academic Journal [Online], Vol 23, 2020, http://journals.openedition.org/samaj/6306.

[3]Preethi Krishnan and MangalaSubramaniam, *Understanding the State: Right to Food Campaign in India,* The Global South,Vol. 8, No. 2, pp. 101-118, Indiana University Press, https://www.jstor.org/stable/10.2979/globalsouth.8.2.101.

[4] Hawkes, Shona, and JagjitKaurPlahe, *Worlds Apart: The WTO's Agreement on Agriculture and the Right to Food in Developing Countries,* International Political Science Review 34.1 (2013) pp. 21–38.

[5] Dan Banik, *The Hungry Nation: Food Policy and Food Politics in India,* Food ethics, Vol 1, 2016, pp.29–45.

CHAPTER THREE

BRIEF SUMMARY

1. **<u>Parliamentary Debates:</u>**

The National Food Security Act, 2013 was greeted with numerous attacks and doubts regarding the ambiguities in the language used, mechanisms for implementing the provisions, potential financial and economic backlash, and so on by all the members of the debate. The bill was discussed by approximately 37 members, plus a few others. This proposal was eventually approved and passed after a long debate which took place for an entire day. wherein the opposition challenged the governing party, claiming that the measure was merely a rehashing and rewording of some previously established schemes and a "gimmick" aimed at upcoming election.It was claimed by a few that this act of promulgating an ordinance just 20 days prior and elections arriving in the near future, the true intention behind such a decision was simply an act of vote bank politics.

This legislation is said to ensure 5 kg of wheat, rice, and crude cereals per head each month at Rs 3, 2, 1 respectively. Even so, in terms of the Public Distribution System, the bill contains numerous deficiencies. There seem to be, for example, states with stronger existing systems, while the bill in question only provides for food grains, whereas other schemes also entail sugar, iodized salt, pulses and other essentials. These states would perform better under the current scheme and must be permitted to continue.The idea of nutrition which is the key element has been ignored.Admittedly, the adoption of the ordinance approach detrimentally limits but doesn't preclude further debate on these and related matters in Parliament. The ordinance brought in reference to the National Food Security Law was argued as a misapplication of the right to introduce ordinance. The opposition clarified that they support the right to food security, however, the manner in which it was brought out warranted suspicion regarding their true intentions.[1] There was another contention that this bill didn't promote the concept of Universal Right to food are an integral part of the debate. As there were multiple categorizations made among the people, while a universal right is one that has to be extended to all equally. It was further criticized as one that could potentially affect the currently well performing "mid-day meal" scheme and would relatively impose a heavier financial burden on BPL families.

Apart from few of the above-mentioned topics of discussion, the following matters were also intensely criticised and deliberated upon with respect to the bill and its functioning during the debates:

- The potent execution of the NFSA persists with states/UTs, and also because governance varies from each state-to-state, the impact of rollout varies as well.
- **Unsatisfactory Transparency:** The NFSA could benefit the wrong people. The classification and recognition of beneficiary households is in the hands of state discretion. In the lack of evident and transparent eligibility requirement, no one has a privilege to any; this subverts the objective of enacting legislation. It was pronounced that the bill was not extended to the needy and deserving, instead reduced/restricted the amount of people who must be covered.

- **PDS leakages:** a leakage indicates that food grains don't reach thetargeted stakeholders. There are 3 forms of leakage which are listed below:

  - During the transit of goods, acts of pilferage.
  - Goods being diverted and given to the rich and those who aren't the original beneficiaries of the scheme.
  - Wilful and intentional embargo of true beneficiaries from the list for allocation.

- **Inadequacy of food grains and storage:** According to international benchmarks, an adult must have 14 kg of food-grains per month, given by ICMR. This legislation allows for just 5 kg of food per person each month. Furthermore, there was a concern regarding the useable storage space/warehouse facilities as the existing facilities would be insufficient for the amount of food grains quoted in the bill for allocation and distribution.[2]

- **Minimum support price:** It has been enunciated in the bill that the MSP would be determined by the state which would result in stripping autonomy from farmers over their produce and living wages culminating in injustice. The welfare of farmers was called into question.
- **Financial and Economic burden:** It was highlighted that there the issue of financial and economic burden on states was not addressed. The additional expenses that must be endured for storage and distribution facilities, constructing more go-downs and establishing PDS stores as well as door-to-door delivery would burden the state.

In response to the multiple concerns raised by the members during the debate, the minister K.V Thomas, Shrimati Sonia Gandhi, others reverted with the following:

The food security legislation is a drop in the bucket compared to what is needed to address India's massive malnutrition. Our nation is experiencing an empowering revolution as a result of this strategy. For the near future, our objective should be to eliminate undernutrition and starvation in our country. Our homeland has been consistently rated very low in the Human Development Index and in meeting Millennium Development Goals. This would augment economic development and lead to a significant decrease in poverty. Access to nutritional food would improve the public's wellbeing.

This bill not only offers food for the destitute, women, and children, but also assists farmers in obtaining an assured support price from the authorities for their harvests.This legislation will not harm farmers because it includes specific arrangements for irrigation and agricultural advancement. Farmers will be provided loans at lower interest rates, as well as suitable MSP. It will also assist to decrease foodgrain spoilage in warehouses.Pregnant women and nursing mothers will be eligible for meals and maternity benefits. Children aged 6 months- 14 years will be eligible for meals through the ICDS and Mid-day Meal Schemes.[3]For the purposes of granting ration cards, the eldest woman in the family who is 18 years or older will be the heads of households.That is, women are elevated to the position of head of family. The bill further will combine numerous welfare measures to include a nutritious element, which will become a law.[4]To minimise financial strain, the Central Government will aid states in reaching expenditures accrued by them for transport facilities of foodgrains. This Bill promotes greater transparency and accountability throughout the PDS scheme.[5] There'll be vigilance and social audit committees. TPDS framework that is entirely secure. 'Food Security Allowance' arrangement: For other concerns, such as financial resources, if the parties do not receive the benefits of this scheme, they will be compensated.

1. **Interpretation as seen in Law Commission Report:**

As explained earlier the NFSA (2013) has been formed with extensive research and analysis. The formation, applicablity,scope,features and meanings have been throughly discussed in the respective Parliamentary debates, Planning comission reports and other discussions. Law Commisssion of India plays the most important part in the drafting and understanding of statutes. The commission very carefully conducts study on the various aspects that come into to play while drafting the statute and also the results once the statute is passed.In case of NFSA (2013), there is no report that has been dedicated solely for the Act. But, the 259th Law Commission Report which is based on Early Childhood Development and Legal Entitlements (August 2015) gives a new light and interpretation of the NSFA (2013).This report was drafted by the 20th Law Commission. The 20th Law Commission of India's Chairman were Justice D.K. Jain from January 2013 to October 2013 and Justice A.P.Shah from November 2013 to August 2015.[6] This report mailnly focused on how the development of young children is recognised as a human rights issue of critical national importance. The report emphasiszes on the statistics on the malnutrition and neglect of young children in India, and their significance for the nation's overall human resources. This report also focuses on rising voices and demanding greater attention from the State on the issue of 'Early Childhood Development (ECD)' that the Government came out with a comprehensive 'Nation Early Childhood Care and Education (ECCE) Policy, 2013'.

Chapter 5 of the report deals with 'Health and Nutrition' under this chapter while talking about major central legeslations dealing with the said topic the report states that Section 4 of the National Food Security Act, 2013 has made provisions recognizing the special needs of pregnant and lactating mother and its relation to child's health. This provision entitles women to "meal, free of charge during pregnancy and six months after the child-birth, through local Anganwadi, so as to meet the nutritional standards specified in Schedule II of the Act."[7]The report further lauds the NFSA(2013) by stating that it is one of the most important step in the positive direction regarding Early Childhood development. It says that this Act significantly recognizes the different needs at different stages of childhood. They expressly mention the importance of Section 5 of the Act stating that specifically gives the meaning of 'entitlementns and what includes the same' which makes the execution of the ECD[8] plans easy. Then, it also mentions Section 6, which is the need for the Anganwadi centers and their role in ECD. Next it mentions how the Act is not limited to children and also extends to providing food security for pregnant and lactating women as present in Section 4 of the Act.

The report then focuses on the implementation part of the respective statutes. It states that the provisions of the NFSA are required to be implemented by the Centre and the States working together. The political consensus to cooperate on this issue has not been fully manifest, neither level has taken sufficient responsibility for implementation, which has thus been inadequate in enforcing the ECD plans efficiently.Later in Chapter 7 which deals with "Conclusions and Recommendations" the commission has expressedits opinion regarding Section 6 of the NFSA(2013). It states that there is a need for evolving guidelines or some methods in order to identify children suffering from malnutrition. They also stated that such and children must be refered to and provided with appropriate healthcare facilities. The comission has suggested that there must be some provision that should be brought so that the nutrition recommendations in Schedule II of the NFSA can be regularly revised in keeping with the latest scientific studies based on calorific value, age, gender and food items respectively.[9]Therefore we can see that the 259th Law Commission Report has analysed the NFSA (2013) in a new light. We can see that the report gives a new perspective of understanding and interpeting the NFSA(2013).

3. <u>Parliamentary Standing Committee Report:</u>

The Bill was referred to the Standing Committee on Food, Consumer Affairs and Public Distribution for examination and report on 5th January 2012 under Rule 331(E) of the Rules of Procedure and Conduct of Business in LokSabha.[10] The resulting report[11] is divided into 3 Chapters and they are discussed below.

Based on the information gathered by the Committee during itsconsultations with various stakeholders, the Committee observed that not a single objection was raised on the Bill per se. However, there are issues such as coverage of beneficiaries in rural and urban areas, identification procedure, exclusion and inclusion criteria, quantum of foodgrains entitlement for priority and general households, nutritional security for women and children, proposal for cash transfer in lieu of foodgrains entitlement and sharing of expenditure by Central and State Governments under various provisions as envisaged in the Bill, etc. on which different views wereexpressed by different sections of the stakeholders.The Committee felt that it is of utmost importance that the Bill remains asimple yet effective framework of the Public Distribution System ensuring food security to the people of India. Itwas also conscious of the large amount of subsidy involved in the implementation of the Bill and was aware that it was likely to increase substantially in the coming years. Accordingly, it noted that it should be the endeavour of the Government to implement the Act in a transparent and efficient manner on a sustainable basis without any adverse implications on the economy.

The Committee further noted that for identification of beneficiaries, the exclusion criteria, inclusion criteria and automatic deprivation indicators prescribed by the Billwere very confusing.It observed that the Bill does not prescribe any scientific or established mechanism for identification of beneficiaries and the multiplicity of categories such as priority households, general households, persons living in starvation, special groups, destitute persons, homeless persons, etc. was bound to lead to several identification errors. It felt that it was not desirable to have multiple categories as mentioned above for inclusion in the Bill as thatwould complicate the identification process. Instead, it advocatedfor an identification process that is fair, transparent, logical and based on a sound rationale. Accordingly, it recommended that the Government may consider devising a clearly defined criteria in consultation with the State Governments for exclusion of 25% population in rural and 50% population in urban areas and the rest of the population should uniformlyget the entitlements without any distinction.The Committee also noted that huge amount of foodgrains are damaged every year due to lack of proper and scientific storage capacity available in the country. Thus, it strongly recommended that the Government should impress upon the FCI, CWC, State Governments, etc.

to cooperate and coordinate with each other and make every effort to create scientific storage capacity not only in procuring States but also in consuming States and other parts of the country for the smooth implementation of the Bill.

Though the previous recommendations made by state governments and other experts suggest that the entitlement to foodgrains under this Act should be a minimum of 7 kg for each person in a month, considering how there could be a shortage in production of foodgrains, the Committee recommended that each person should be entitled to 5 kg in a month so that the target set by the Act is practical. The Committee defended the shift of foodgrains entitlement from household basis to per person basis as put forward in the Bill by stating that households with a larger number of members would now be able to get larger quantity of foodgrains. The Committee observed that the Bill made provisions for giving a free meal to pregnant women and children below two years of age at Anganwadi but the Committee felt that this is impractical as Anganwadis are not present in all parts of the country and even in places where they are functioning, it would be difficult for pregnant women and children below two years to go there for the free meal. The Committee instead recommended that pregnant women be given an extra 5 kg of foodgrains per month in addition to what they were already entitled to until two years are completed after childbirth. Because of this additional entitlement and the impracticality of children below the age of two years to go to Anganwadis for a free meal as proposed by the Bill, the Committee recommended that the free meal need not be provided for children below the age of two years and pregnant women. But the Committee recommended that once children start going to school, till the age of sixteen, they be given one free meal daily at their school run by the government or government-aided schools.

[1]RajyaSabha, https://rajyasabha.nic.in/rsnew/publication_electronic/National_Food_security_Act2013.pdf(last visited Feb. 2, 2022).

[2]Ibid.

[3]Shakeel A. RECENT TRENDS IN THE DEBATE ON INDIA'S NATIONAL FOOD SECURITY ACT (NFSA) – 2013: TRAGEDY OR TRIUMPH? *GEOGRAPHY, ENVIRONMENT, SUSTAINABILITY.* ISSN 2542-1565 (Online)2018;11(2):108-124. https://doi.org/10.24057/2071-9388-2018-11-2-108-124.

[4]Supra note 1.

[5]Ibid 4.

[6]Legal Affairs, https://legalaffairs.gov.in/sites/default/files/ LAW%20COMMISSION%20OF%20INDIA.pdf (last visited Feb. 2, 2022).

[7] National Food Security Act 2013, S.4, No. 20, Acts of Parliament, 2013 (India).

[8] National Food Security Act 2013, S.5, No. 20, Acts of Parliament, 2013 (India).

[9]Law Commission of India, https://lawcommissionofindia.nic.in/ reports/Report259.pdf (last visited Feb. 2, 2022).

[10]LokSabha Secretariat,*Rules of Procedure and Conduct in the LokSabha*, (April 2014) http://164.100.47.194/loksabha/rules/ RULES-2010-P-FINAL_1.pdf(last visited Feb. 2, 2022).

[11]Standing CommitteeonFood, Consumer Affairs and Public Distribution (2012-13), *Twenty Seventh Report - National Food Security Bill of 2011*(January 2013).

CHAPTER FOUR

ANALYSIS

The pre-existing socio-economic prejudices in the Indian society are a fraud on the people's fundamental rights. The same differences even affect the political will to implement certain beneficial acts. One such act which was driven with much political fiasco is the NFSA. Despite the fault-finding opposition against the act, this particular statute proved to be beneficial to the people. There were many early setbacks due to lack of implementationand institutional bias but the act trumped all of that to give the entitlements it guaranteed. With the enactment of NFSA, India has joined the club of countries with a dedicated legislation to food security. The act is a watershed development in the path to realise right to food. But the most notable character of the act is timeline it was implemented in. The act was implemented after the apex court held all the schemes included in the act as legal entitlements. In such background the purpose and the will of the act becomes unclear. The interaction of multi-dimensional facets of food security call for a legal backing and that is where NFSA fills the gap. There are many instruments to analysea socio-welfare legislation like NFSA:

- **Historical Setting:** The journey to attainment of self-sufficiency in food grains production at the national level has been a tough one. The green revolution helped to revive from the hunger deaths and famines, but we needed a long-term solution and NFSA was that solution. India's public distribution system is one of the largest structural distribution systems for food grains in the world. There are many issues at each level and a legislationwill resolve such issues by providing alternative mechanisms. In order to address the food security at household level the government came up with the idea of targeted public distribution system (TPDS) for BPL which also includes Antyodya Anna Yojana (AAY) and Above Poverty Line (APL). NFSA gives the much needed legal backing to the existing TPDS. The proposed NFSA legislation marks a paradigm shift in addressing the problem of food security from the then welfare approach to a rights based approach. Under the new approach, about two thirds of the population will be entitled to receive subsidized food grains under Targeted Public Distribution System. The legislation was to also confer legal rights on women, especially pregnant and lactating women; and children; and other special groups such as tribal and forest dwellers, destitute, homeless, disaster and emergency affected persons and persons living in starvation, to receive meal free of charge or at affordable price, as the case maybe.

Below table shows the timeline of NFSA.

Evolution of PDS	Timeline	Details
PDS	1940s	Launched as general entitlement scheme
TPDS	1997	PDS was revamped to target poor households
Antyodaya Anna Yojana	2000	Scheme launched to target the poorest of the poor
PDS Control Order	2001	Government notified this Order administer TPDS
PUCL vs Union of India	2001	Ongoing case in Supreme Court contending that "right to food" is a fundamental right
National Food Security Act	2013	Act to provide legal right to food to the poor

- **Objective:** The objective of the act is to provide food and nutritional security in human life-cycle based approach, by ensuring access to adequate quantity of quality of food at affordable prices to people to live a life with dignity.[1]The schemes for a life-cycle approach were given legal backing in the PUCL case by the apex court. The same were further substantiated and made into justiciable rights by the NFSA. There are eight schemes for the life-cycle approach they also include: Mid-Day Meal Scheme, and Integrated Child Development Services (ICDS) for children and infants respectively, the Anganwadi schemes, maternity benefits, TPDS and AAY provide right to food as a fundamental right to all people at all levels.
- **Features:** The salient features of the act signify what the act should do and whether it should have beneficial construction and liberal interpretation when questioned. NFSA being welfare legislation should be interpreted for the benefit of the people and to suppress the mischief and advance the remedy. There are many features in the act hat advanced the existing systems to a greater coverage and the cope was more

inclusive than the previous schemes. The salient features include:

- major change to the TPDS provisions, the TPDS scheme was an administrative system now made into a legal entitlement, TPDS was extended to more people who are in dire need.

Below table shows the comparative position of TPDS.

Table I Comparison of TPDS provisions before and after NFSA			
Provisions		Pre-NFSA	Post-NFSA
Coverage (by Central Government)		BPL Population (29.5% in 2011-12)	813.4 million (75% in Rural Areas and 50% in Urban Areas)
Selection Criteria		Below Poverty Line (BPL) Survey – 2002 (Rural) and 2007 (Urban)	Determined by State Government
Quantity of Rations	APL	15 kg (depending on availability)	Excluded
	BPL (Priority)	35 kg	5 kg per member
	AAY (AAY)	35 kg	35 kg
Price of Food Items (per kg)	APL	Rice – Rs. 8.30; Wheat – Rs. 6.10	Excluded
	BPL (Priority)	Rice – Rs. 5.65; Wheat – Rs. 4.15; Coarse Grains – Rs. 3	Rice – Rs. 3; Wheat – Rs. 2; Coarse Grains – Rs. 1
	AAY (AAY)	Rice – Rs. 3; Wheat – Rs. 2	

- Women empowerment by making them the heads of the houses for ration card issuance.
- Identification of the households based on TPDS for BPL and AAY for the poorest of the poor sections[1]
- Food Security allowance in case the adequate food grains not provided.[2]
- And any other schemes as deemed fit, penalty for violation of the act and grievance redressal mechanism.

On the whole the provisions and the features signify the importance of a separate legislation. The effects can also be seen from the global hunger index of India. The hunger index went from alarming to serious. By avoiding the existing implementation gaps and mending the ways of the governments at each level NFSA can be a revolutionary regime to create and realize the fundamental right to food and live with dignity. The fundamental problem of hunger is rooted in the problem of access to food grains. There is a huge gap between the buffer stocks available and the distribution of the food grains. Legislations like a NFSA create a duty on the state for timely distribution of the available food grains in turn strengthening the food security. With NFSA there are huge chances of poverty alleviation and other such problems. Schemes which provide employment need longer time for realization but distribution of food grains show the immediate rise in the nutritional and living standards of the people. Hunger is the ground zero level, with an empty stomach there is no capacity to do work and earn and it ultimately effects the development. So NFSA tries to overcome the problem from the grass root level by filling the starved stomachs.

[1] National Food Security Act 2013, S. 9,10(1)(a),(b), No. 20, Acts of Parliament, 2013 (India).

[2] National Food Security Act 2013, S.8, No. 20, Acts of Parliament, 2013 (India).

[1] National Food Security Act 2013, No. 20, Acts of Parliament, 2013 (India).

CHAPTER FIVE

CONCLUSION

NFSA has been one of those acts which was hugely discussed over the media, in the parliament and every socio-political and economical platform when it was enacted. Some call it a huge burden on the government but others see it as a solution to the primal problem of hunger. Acts like NFSA should not fall into the wrong set of concerns. The implementation loopholes are common in every regime but on the bright side the act provides a systematic way to distribute the food grains and consolidates the multiple overlapping schemes through life-cycle approach. There is always a possible misstep in the implementation of large-scale transfers in a country like India but there is a beneficial side to the acts like NFSA which cannot be ignored. The massive historical background of NFSA further emphasises the significance of the act. Interpretative instruments can analyse the act in a multi-faceted way thereby highlighting the intention and purpose of the legislation. Such interpretative instruments therefore can further help to overcome the implementation gaps and accelerate the realisation of true potential of the beneficial legislations like NFSA.